Built From Scratch

Affiliate Income
for
Beginners

by

Brian Turner

First Edition
2025

First Edition

ISBN: 979-8-9995161-5-2

BUILT FROM SCRATCH: Affiliate Income for Beginners

This book is intended for informational purposes only. The author and publisher are not engaged in rendering legal, financial, or other professional advice. Readers should consult qualified professionals before making business or financial decisions.

Table of Contents

INTRO – Accidental Income

This isn't magic. It's math.
A link, a click, a commission. That's it.
I was getting paid to book my own travel
for years. No strategy, no marketing, just
a quiet little banner doing work in the
background.
Once I figured that out, I stopped
treating affiliate income like a side hustle
and started treating it like a system.

You won't find screenshots of six-figure
dashboards, or promises of passive
income while you sleep.
What you will find is *game you can
actually use*.
Real tools. Real lessons. Real wins — and
real Ls — from someone who figured it
out mid-hustle.

There's a lot of noise out there.
Affiliate courses. Fluffy blog posts. Flashy
dashboards. AI-written ebooks that all
say the same thing.
This isn't that.

I wrote this for the builders.
The ones trying to earn a little more,
stretch what they have, or create
something out of nothing.
The ones who've been hustling... but just
needed a system that made sense.

One of my first real lessons? Expedia.

I had this little affiliate banner on one of
my old sites. No email list. No sales
funnel. I just used it to book my own
travel. But then the checks started
coming in.

At first, I thought it was a fluke. But the
more I booked... the more I got paid.
Turns out, I was sending traffic to
Expedia — even if that traffic was just *me*.
And yep, I got the commission. Every
time.

I became an Expedia Platinum member
without even realizing it. Between
affiliate payouts, hotel upgrades, and
credit card points? I was doing *pretty
good* just doing what I love — traveling,
building, moving.

*(For context: Expedia pays around 10%
commission on hotel bookings through
their affiliate program on CJ. A $500 stay*

could earn you $50 — plus reward points, perks, and credit card bonuses if you're stacking it right. That adds up fast.)

The crazy part? I already knew affiliate marketing worked.
I'd seen the money come in.
But as much as I've done, as much as I've built — I was intimidated by it.

I never really took the time to learn. Never built a system. Never scaled anything.
And because of that? I left *so much* money on the table. Missed out on so many chances to turn clicks into cash.

When I restarted recently — for real this time — I couldn't believe how easy the Amazon Affiliates program is now.
It wasn't like that when I first started years ago. The game has changed. It's more accessible. And now that I'm actually focused, the results are showing up *faster* than I expected.

Here's what I've learned:
Most people quit because they don't see results fast enough.
Not because affiliate marketing doesn't work, but because they never had a system that *did*.

And if I already had a system that made money without trying...
Then, putting real structure and simple marketing behind it?
My income potential doesn't just improve — it multiplies.

This book won't just help you make a few dollars — it might be the reason your podcast pays for itself, or your content starts covering your bills.
It might even be the spark that replaces your income completely.

That's what this is about.
Not hype. Not theory.
Just a real builder's guide to making your first (or next) dollar with affiliate income — from scratch.

If that sounds like you... keep reading.

Chapter 1 – The Truth About Affiliate Marketing

Before we dive into strategies and tools, we need to clear something up:
Affiliate marketing isn't a magic trick.
It's not a secret hack.
And it's definitely not a business in a box.

What it *is* — is a way to earn money by recommending things you already use, believe in, or already talk about.

It's a commission check for doing what people already do every day: sharing links, giving advice, and pointing others toward the products or services they need.

What It *Really* Is

At the core, affiliate marketing is simple:

1. You sign up for a program (Amazon, Expedia, Shopify, etc.)

2. They give you a unique link.

3. Someone clicks your link and makes a purchase.

4. You get paid.

That's it: A link, a click, a commission. But just because it's simple doesn't mean it's easy.

Affiliate marketing is not:

- "Post a few links and get rich."

- "Set it and forget it."

- "Passive income... with zero effort."

That's what most people get wrong — and why most people give up before they ever make a dollar.

Three Big Myths That Block Beginners

Myth #1: You need a huge following.
Nope. A focused strategy with 20 clicks will beat random links in front of 2,000 people every time. Micro audiences convert better when you show up with trust.

Myth #2: You have to fake being a "content creator."
You don't need a podcast, blog, or YouTube channel

(yet)
You need a platform — even if it's just your IG bio or Linktree page — and a reason someone should click.

Myth #3: You only make pennies.
Yes, Amazon pays low percentages (3–10%), but other platforms pay $50, $100, and even recurring commissions.
The key is recommending what actually fits your life, and your audience's.

Why Most Beginners Fail

They:

- Sign up for too many programs too fast

- Promote products they don't use or trust

- The don't track what's working

- Expect money by the weekend

Affiliate income is earned, not promised.
You're not selling products — you're selling trust.
And trust takes time, consistency, and honesty.

The Shift That Changes Everything

Stop thinking like a seller.
Start thinking like a recommender.

If a friend asked, "What laptop should I buy?"
You'd probably link them to the one you use, right?

Affiliate marketing is just putting a simple system
behind that same energy — and getting paid for it.

Real Talk: What Made It Click for Me

Whenever we booked family trips — or I traveled
with the homies — I'd drop my Expedia link in the
group chat and say:
"Be sure to use this when you book."

And when they did?
Those checks hit different.

I was making affiliate money off trips I was already
taking.
Stacking points. Cashing perks. Getting paid, off
something I was doing anyway.

And the wild part?
I didn't even realize how much I was leaving on the
table.

Truth is... I was too busy chasing other plays.
Too distracted to double down on what was quietly
working.
Too unaware of the opportunity sitting in plain sight.

I didn't understand how big affiliate programs could get.
Didn't realize how far one link could go.
Didn't treat it like income — just a bonus.

But let me tell you —
when life humbles you,
when money gets tight,
when $100 means keeping the lights on...

That extra commission check?
It's not play money — it's breathing room.

That's when it clicked:
If one link could do that casually...
Imagine what a system could do *intentionally*.

You don't need more noise.
You need a system.
And that's what we're building in the next chapter.

Chapter 2 – The Tools That Actually Matter

You don't need a fancy setup to start earning affiliate income.
But you do need a *foundation*.

There's a difference between being active... and being aligned.
And if you know me, you already know — the goal is to be **Aligned AF**.

Because when your tools, brand, and income streams line up — that's when things start working on purpose.
That's when things start working *on purpose*.

The Core Four

You can run this game with just four main tools.
Everything else is extra. Let's keep it simple.

---

1. Link Manager
Where your affiliate links live — short, clean, and trackable.

Use: Pretty Links (WordPress), Bitly, TinyURL

Why: You want clean links like `heybbt.com/tools/AirPods` instead of messy Amazon URLs.

Bonus: Lets you update a link once and change its destination later, without reposting it everywhere.

---

2. Content Hub

Where you send people — your affiliate "home base."

Options: Linktree, Stan.store, or a "Tools I Use" page

Why: This is your storefront. Your digital shelf. Your highlight reel.

How I use it: Banners at the top, featured tools below, rotating offers as needed.

---

3. Email List (Optional but Powerful)

Where you build trust and follow up without the algorithm.

Use: ConvertKit, MailerLite, or Flodesk

Why: Email builds relationship — and gives you direct access to your audience.

How to start: Offer a simple freebie ("Get my free guide") → send a few value-packed follow-up emails → drop in a relevant affiliate offer.

---

4. Tracking + Payout Dashboards
Where you monitor what's working — and what's paying.

Use: CJ, Impact, Amazon Associates, Shopify, etc.

Why: You need to track clicks, commissions, and top-performing links to grow.

Pro tip: Check weekly, not hourly. Don't chase noise — look for patterns that scale.

Real Talk: My Original Stack

When I finally stopped playing around and got serious, this is what I started with:

- **Pretty Links** (on my WordPress blog)

- **Linktree Pro** (with branded banners and affiliate sections)

- **CJ + Amazon** (where most of my early income came from)

- **No email list yet** — just smart placement and consistency

I made my first intentional affiliate dollars from tools I already used in real life.
Apple AirPods. My podcast mic. Expedia. Canva. Shopify.

No pitch. Just a link.
No funnel. Just a recommendation.

I remember one of my earlier checks.
I remember one of my early checks — I logged in and saw an extra $400 sitting there.
That one payout allowed me to upgrade to a nicer hotel during my next trip.
No launch. No sale. Just a link — quietly doing work in the background.

You Don't Need to Be "Techy" — You Just Need Structure

This game isn't about being the smartest or flashiest.
It's about being *organized* and *intentional*.

- If you've got one solid tool page...

- One smart link in your bio...

- One product you can stand behind...

You can make money. Consistently.

Next, I'll show you how to choose the right products. But don't skip this step. Tools don't just make it easier — they make it *possible*.

Get your setup right — even if it's basic.

Because the same system that earns $10 can scale to $1,000 and beyond.

That's the play.

Chapter 3 – Products You Can Actually Stand Behind

One of the biggest mistakes beginners make is chasing commission instead of choosing alignment.

They promote products they don't use.
Sign up for every program they can find.
Start pushing links that don't even make sense for their audience — or their brand.

That's not how we move.

If you want long-term affiliate income — the kind that shows up even when you're not posting — the product has to make sense in your life first.

You need to be able to stand behind it.

Use + Recommend Only

Here's the simple rule I live by:

If I wouldn't use it, I won't recommend it.

If I wouldn't send it to a friend, it doesn't get the link.

The moment you start promoting just for the payout is the moment people stop trusting you. And once trust is gone, the clicks dry up.

You don't need a million options.
You just need a few products that feel real — that match how you live, build, and move.

Where to Find Affiliate Programs That Fit You

Start with what you already use. Seriously — look around you.

- **Do you use Amazon?** (They have an affiliate program for almost everything.)

- **Do you book travel?** (Expedia, Booking.com, TripAdvisor — all pay.)

- **Do you host a website or run a store?** (Shopify, GoDaddy, Bluehost, etc.)

- **Do you use business tools?** (ConvertKit, Flodesk, Thinkific, or QuickBooks.)

- **Do you buy tech or gear?** (Apple, Best Buy, Sweetwater, Logitech.)

You're already a customer — you just haven't been getting paid for it.

Major Affiliate Networks to Explore

If you're ready to expand, here are the networks I personally use or recommend:

- **CJ (Commission Junction):** Great for Expedia, Office Depot, GoDaddy, and more

- **Impact:** Shopify, Flodesk, ConvertKit, and digital tools

- **Partnerize:** Retail brands and niche products

- **Amazon Associates:** Low commissions, but easy to use and highly trusted

- **ShareASale:** Great for home, lifestyle, fashion, and small brands

- **Rakuten Advertising:** Big-name retailers like Walmart, Macy's, and Best Buy

Tip: Don't sign up for everything at once.

Pick 2–3 that match your lane, and start slow.

Real Talk: My First Stack

When I got serious about affiliate income, I stopped chasing everything — and just promoted what I actually used:

- **Expedia** (I was traveling anyway)

- **AirPods and tech gear** via Amazon

- **Shopify** (because I was building stores)

- **Flodesk + ConvertKit** (for email)

No scripts. No pressure. I just told people:
"This is what I use — here's the link."

The first time someone asked,
"What mic do you use for your podcast?"
I sent them the link. That was it. One click. One payout.

Personal L: What I Did Wrong

When I first signed up with CJ, I was signing up for every advertiser that would accept me, not knowing what I was doing.

I was throwing links all over my site — hoping something would hit.

No strategy. No trust. No results.

I wasn't promoting products I actually used.
I was just chasing programs.
And that never works.

Don't do what I did.

Start slow. Start with what you know. Build trust before traffic.

The "Always Use" Checklist

Before you promote anything, ask yourself:

- Have I used this product personally?

- Would I recommend it to someone I care about?

- Can I explain what it is and why it works for me — without sounding like a salesperson?

- Would I feel comfortable seeing my name attached to it publicly?

If the answer isn't **yes** to all four... don't promote it.

It's not just about the check.
It's about the brand you're building.

Your Personal Affiliate Product List

Take 5 minutes. List out products you already use, love, or talk about often.

Pick 3 from your list and apply to their affiliate programs today.

Don't overthink it — just get started.

Chapter 4 – Where to Place Your Links

Having affiliate links is one thing.
Getting people to click them — that's the game.

Most beginners mess this part up.

They either:

- Spam links everywhere and lose trust

- Hide them so well no one ever clicks

- Or never give people a *reason* to care in the first place

This chapter is about placing your links *with purpose*, not pressure.

Your Links Need a Home

The #1 mistake I made early on? Not having a consistent place to send people.

I'd post a link here, drop one there — and by the next day, I couldn't even remember where I put anything.

That's why you need a **primary link hub** — a single place where your affiliate links live.

Smart Places to Put Your Links

Let's break down the real spots where your links can live, without looking desperate or random.

---

1. Link-in-Bio Tools (Linktree, Stan.store, etc.)

Your bio is prime real estate. People click when they're curious — give them something worth landing on.

What to include:

- Featured affiliate tools (rotate often)

- A "Tools I Use" section

- Your ebook, podcast, or store (if you have one)

How I use it:

- I add branded banners (like "My Podcast Mic" or "Gear I Use") so people know what they're clicking before they even open the page.

---

2. "Tools I Use" or "Builder's Kit" Page

This is your affiliate shelf — where everything you recommend is clearly listed.

Each product should have:

- A short explanation

- The link

- And maybe a "why I use it" one-liner

Keep it clean. Keep it current.

---

3. Content Descriptions (Podcast, YouTube, Blog)

Any time you create content, give the people what they need.

If you mention a product in a podcast or video, link it in the description.
Every time.

You don't have to sound like an ad. Just be real:

> "I recorded this episode using [insert mic name] — you can grab it here if you're building your own setup."

Simple. Non-pushy. Useful.

---

4. Inside Your Products (eBooks, Checklists, Courses)

If someone downloaded your freebie or bought your ebook, that means they trust you.

That's the perfect moment to recommend something that can help them even more.

I've used affiliate links inside:

- My ebooks

- PDF worksheets

- Email autoresponders

- Bonus resource lists

It's passive, but powerful.

---

5. Social Media Captions + Stories

You don't have to promote every day. But when it fits, make the link count.

Try captions like:

> "A few of y'all asked about what I use to record podcast episodes. I dropped the link in bio."

Or in stories:

> "This is the mic I use. Affiliate link in my tools page. Changed my audio game."

You're not forcing it — you're just pointing people toward value.

Real Talk: What I Did Wrong

I was definitely a spammer.
Whether I was emailing or dumping links all over my website, I was just pushing out as much info as possible, thinking *somebody* had to click it.

Boy, was I wrong.

When I think about the old me, I'm like,
"You big ole dummy."

I really thought affiliate marketing was magic.

Like if I hit enough people, somebody would find it and buy.

Nah. That's not how trust works.

When you're all over the place, people don't care.

I had no system, no focus, and no strategy.
And that's exactly what I got back in return: no clicks, no sales, no income.

The BBT Link Strategy

Here's how I keep it simple now:

1. **Linktree Pro** — One hub with rotating banners and a "Builder Tools" section

2. **Visit: heybbt.com/tools** — A clean, branded tools page with everything I actually use

3. **Descriptions** — Every YouTube video, podcast episode, and ebook includes relevant links

4. **Instagram bio + stories** — I update these when I highlight something specific

Now my system works without me chasing.

People know where to go.

And if they're ready? They click.

Don't Make It Complicated — Make It Clear

Affiliate income isn't about chasing people.
It's about helping the people who are already
watching, listening, reading, or building with you.

When someone asks what you use, your link should
already be ready.

That's the shift:

Stop asking, "How do I promote this?"

Start asking, "Where does this link naturally fit into
what I already do?"

Next up, we'll talk about making that **first real
commission** — and what to do after that first win
hits.

Chapter 5 – Making That First Commission

This is the part everybody waits for.
That first notification.
That first payout.
That moment where it finally clicks:
"This actually works."

But most people never get there.

Not because affiliate marketing doesn't work — but because most people don't stick with it long enough to see the reward.

So let's make sure you do.

What That First Win Really Looks Like

Let's be honest:
Your first commission might only be $2.57.
It might be $14.60.
It might be $50 if you promote the right offer.

And that's fine — because the goal isn't to get rich overnight.
The goal is to **get proof**.

Once you know how to generate $1 on purpose...

you can figure out how to earn $10, then $100 — and scale from there.

The "First Win Funnel" – A Simple 3-Step Path

Here's the fastest, cleanest way to make your first affiliate commission:

Step 1: Pick One Product You Use and Trust

You already did this in Chapter 3 — now choose one that:

- Is affordable (under $100 works best)

- Solves a clear problem

- Feels natural for your audience

Think: "What's something I've talked about this week already?"

Step 2: Create One Piece of Content Around It

This doesn't have to be viral.

You just need a real recommendation in one of these formats:

- **IG story:** "This saved me so much time. Links's in the tools page."

- **Blog post:** "Here are three tools I use to record my podcast."

- **Podcast/YouTube episode:** "I use this mic — affiliate link in the description."

- **Email:** "A few of y'all asked what I use — here it is."

You're not selling — you're explaining.

Step 3: Share the Link Strategically

Place it:

- In your Tools I Use page

- In your Linktree

- In your description or pinned comment

- In your caption or story, with a clear call to action

Bonus Tip:
If allowed by the affiliate program, consider buying a product you already use using your own link.

That can be a quick win — but only if the affiliate
program terms allow it.

Real Talk: Be Careful With Self-Purchases

It might seem smart to use your own affiliate link
when buying something for yourself or your
business.
And in some cases, it works.

But not all programs allow it.

Amazon is strict.
If they catch you using your own affiliate link to buy
products, they'll shut down your account without
warning.
That's not theory — that's real.

Some creators learned the hard way:
They were buying business gear with their own link,
thinking they'd earn a little cashback.

Next thing they knew — banned.

Check the terms.
Don't lose long-term income for short-term gain.

Real Talk: My First On-Purpose Commission

I don't remember the exact moment of my first affiliate payout — not fully.

However, I do remember realizing that money had quietly appeared in my account...
and it came from a product I was already using, already talking about, already living with.

No special campaign. No launch. Just a link — doing its job.

That was the moment I stopped seeing affiliate marketing as a side hustle...
and started seeing it as a system I could trust.

What to Expect (So You Don't Quit)

Your first commission might come fast.
Or it might take a few days.
But here's what you can control:

- Your consistency

- Your clarity

- Your placement

- Your follow-through

You don't need hundreds of clicks — you need intentional ones.
And they come from trust, not traffic.

The Check That Hits Different

When you see that first payout — even if it's just $10 — something changes.

You stop guessing.
You stop wondering.
You start building on what works.

Because now?
You've done it once.
You can do it again.

First Commission Tracker

Step	Details
Product Chosen	_____
Content Type (Post, Email, Video, etc.)	_____

Where You Shared It   _____

Link Used   _____

Date Posted   _____

First Commission Earned   _____

What Worked?   _____

Would You Do It Again? (Why or   _____
Why Not)

In the next chapter, we'll talk about turning one commission into something more consistent. Because this isn't a fluke — it's a system.

Chapter 6 – What to Do Next

So you made your first commission.

That win was important — not just for your pocket, but for your *confidence*.
But now comes the part most beginners miss:

What do you do next?

You don't double down randomly — you build intentionally.

You shift from accidental to aligned.

From Link to Leverage

That first commission?
It proved one thing: people trust you enough to click and buy.

Now the question is:

How do you earn that trust more often — without constantly posting or begging for attention?

Here's your roadmap:

Step 1: Double Down on What Worked

Look at the product that converted:

- What problem did it solve?

- Who needed it?

- Where did you post it?

- What format got attention — email, video, IG, blog?

Now replicate the structure — don't rebuild the wheel.

You're not guessing anymore.
You're reverse-engineering what actually worked — and turning it into a repeatable system.

Step 2: Build a Simple System (That You Can Repeat)

Here's a quick system you can repeat weekly or monthly:

1. One product you use
2. One piece of content around it
3. One link placement that makes sense

4. One follow-up or reminder (story post, DM, email nudge)

That's a system.
Not hustle. Not guessing.
Just real content with a real offer — done consistently.

> **Your friends and family might support you early on, but they're not your target market..**
> Relying on them too much will throw you off track.
> You're building a system for real growth, not just one-time favors.

Step 3: Create a "Tools I Use" Page (If You Haven't Yet)

If you don't have one already, this is your next move.

It's not just a landing page — it's a silent sales team.

Name it something that fits your vibe:

- "What I Use to Build"

- "My Go-To Tools"

- "Creator Essentials"

- "Digital Toolbox"

Then add it to:

- Your IG or Linktree

- Your blog or website menu

- Your email signature

- Your YouTube or podcast description

Step 4: Create Evergreen Content

Now that you've proven it works, think long-term.

- Write a blog post that'll still be relevant 6 months from now

- Record a short video breaking down why you love a tool

- Pin your best-performing post or make a highlight of your go-to links

- Turn your FAQs or most common DMs into a content series — "Here's what I use."

You're building assets — not just chasing clicks.

What Is Evergreen Content?

If you're new to this, you might be asking:

"What does 'evergreen' even mean?"

Evergreen content is content that stays fresh, no matter when someone finds it.
It's not tied to trends, holidays, or news. It stays useful.

Think:

- A guide to setting up affiliate links

- A list of tools you use to build your business

- A review of your favorite software or mic

These are the types of posts that:

- Keep getting searched

- Keep getting shared

- Keep earning your affiliate income... long after you've moved on

When we say "build evergreen," we mean: create content that works even when you're offline.

That's how you make this sustainable.

Step 5: Don't Go Wild... Yet

This is where people mess up.

They get a $20 payout and suddenly apply to every
affiliate program on the planet.
That's not strategy — that's spam energy.

Stick with:

- Products you use

- Platforms you understand

- Audiences you serve

Scale slowly. Stay aligned.

Brand Over Side Hustle

Here's the truth most people miss:

The money is cool, but the brand is what scales.

If affiliate income always feels like a side hustle,
you'll treat it like one — and your audience will, too.

But when you align your links with your mission?
When your tools reflect your values?
When your content helps without feeling like a sales pitch?

That's when it becomes part of the brand.
That's when you stop chasing commissions and start building equity.

> *"How do you make this feel like part of your brand — not just a random link?"*

It starts with alignment.

It grows with consistency.

And it scales with story — the story behind why you use what you use.

We'll unpack this even deeper in the online course and the next book.
But for now, just remember:
This isn't about selling. It's about service.

My Personal Strategy After That First Win

After that first affiliate payout hit, I didn't launch a big campaign.

I sat down, pulled out a notebook, and wrote three things:

1. What did I just do that worked?

2. How could I make it easier to do again?

3. How do I make this feel like *part of my brand*, not a random side hustle?

That's when the whole game changed.

I wasn't just a content creator.
I was a builder.

System Builder Worksheet

System Element	Notes
Best Product That Converted	_____
Type of Content That Worked	_____
Best Platform / Channel	_____
Audience / Problem It Solved	_____
Link Placement	_____
Call-to-Action Used	_____
What to Repeat Next Time	_____

In the next chapter, we'll talk about how to structure your content and link placements — without feeling like you're always selling.

Chapter 7 – Smart Content, Smarter Links

At this point, most people make one of two mistakes:

1. **They post nonstop about products, and lose trust.**

2. **They don't post at all — and miss out on money.**

The truth is: affiliate marketing isn't about spamming your followers.
It's about telling the right story — in the right format — with the right link.

Let's talk about how to do it right.

The Link Isn't the Strategy. The Story Is.

Before you share a link, ask yourself:
What's the story behind this product?

- Did it solve a problem for you?

- Did it replace something that wasn't working?

- Did it save you time, money, or frustration?

That's what people care about. Not specs. Not affiliate codes.
They want to know: *"Why this one?"*

Your story is the sale.

The Formats That Work

You don't need to go viral. You need to be valuable. Here are simple, proven formats that convert:

- **"What I Use" Lists**
  ("Here's everything I used to build this project.")

- **Tool Breakdowns**
  ("This is the mic I use for my podcast and why")

- **Before + After**
  ("I used to struggle with ___. Then I found ___.")

- **FAQ Answers**
  ("People keep asking me about my setup.

Here's what I use.")

- **Comparison Posts**
  ("I tested three platforms. Here's what I stuck with.")

- **Behind-the-Scenes**
  ("This is how I actually built that thing you saw me post.")

Don't overthink it. Teach people what helped you, and give them the link to do it themselves.

Content First → Link Second

Here's a quick filter I use before sharing any affiliate link:

- **What am I already talking about?**

- **What helped me with that topic?**

- **Can I teach it or tell a story around it?**

- **Now, where should I place the link?**

This keeps you from sounding like a walking ad.
It makes your recommendations feel natural — like part of the conversation, not a pitch.

Quick Interlude — Let Me Be Real

I'll be real with you — this ain't my favorite part either.
Talking links, formats, and placements... it always felt boring.
I'm a builder. I'd rather just *do the thing* and keep it moving.

But I had to learn this:

> **If you're gonna make real money from affiliate marketing, you can't skip the setup.**

You don't have to love marketing, but you gotta respect the system.
Because the right story + the right content + the right link = consistent commissions.

And once you figure that out?
You can scale it without posting every day.

That's the goal.

Where to Drop Your Links (Without Being Spammy)

Website or Blog

- "Tools" page

- Footer section

- Inline product mentions in blog posts

- Banner in your sidebar or homepage

Email

- Welcome email ("Tools I Recommend")

- Signature ("Built this using these tools")

- Tips series with soft mentions

Social Media

- IG Highlights ("My Tools" or "What I Use")

- Linktree / bio tools

- Story replies (only when relevant)

- Content pinned to your profile

YouTube or Podcast

- Description box

- "Gear I Use" section

- Shoutouts inside the content

Remember: **your goal isn't to force the link — it's to place it where it belongs.**
Put it where people are already curious or asking questions.

My Early Mistake: The Spammy Link Phase

Early on, I thought, "If I put more links out, I'll make more money."
So I dropped links in random blog posts. I emailed people who didn't ask.
I was basically the affiliate version of a robocall.

It didn't work.

Nobody likes being sold to constantly, especially not by someone they trust.

> **Here's the shift:**
> If it feels like a recommendation, people lean in.
> If it feels like a pitch, people scroll past.

The Trust Formula

Trust = Realness + Relevance + Repetition

- **Realness:** Be honest about your experience

- **Relevance:** Only promote what fits your content or audience

- **Repetition:** Don't be afraid to share again in new ways

Affiliate income grows when people believe you. And people believe you when they feel like you're *helping*, not just selling.

Final Thought: Don't Let the Link Do All the Work

The link might earn the money —
but the *content earns the click*.

When you share with purpose...
When you educate instead of sell...
When you show how something fits into your real life...

That's when affiliate marketing feels good.
That's when it becomes a business.

Chapter 8 – Your 3-Part Affiliate Content Plan

Most people never make affiliate income because they never make a plan.
They post once. Maybe twice. Then wonder why they're not getting clicks.

> **Posting once and praying is not a strategy — it's a screenshot and a silent timeline.**

This chapter changes that.

By the end of this chapter, you'll have a simple system you can repeat weekly — without sounding like a salesperson or burning out your audience.

Step 1: Choose a Product or Tool You Believe In

This is the foundation.

Start with something you **actually use** or **genuinely recommend.**
Affiliate marketing works best when it feels real, because it *is* real.

Quick filters to help you choose:

- Do I use this regularly?

- Did it save me time, money, or frustration?

- Have I recommended it before (even without a link)?

- Would I still share this if I didn't get paid?

Start there.

Step 2: Pick 3 Styles of Content to Build Around It

You don't need 30 posts.
You need 3 *styles* of content that hit different angles — and feel natural to you.

Here's a simple model:

---

1. Story Content (Connection)

Show how the product fits into your life.
Examples:

- "I remember struggling with ___ until I found ___."

- "Funny story — I actually bought this by accident..."

- "Here's how this one tool saved me hours."

The goal: human connection.

---

2. Value Content (Education)

Break down what it is and why it helps.
Examples:

- "Top 3 features that made this worth it"

- "This vs. that: Why I picked ___"

- "What to know before buying ___"

The goal: teach, don't sell.

---

3. Direct Content (Call-to-Action)

Be upfront — but still helpful.
Examples:

- "I use this every day. Here's the link."

- "A few people asked about my setup — here's the full list."

- "If you're looking for ___, this is my go-to."

The goal: make it easy to take action.

Step 3: Publish, Track, Repeat

Once you post, **watch what works.**
Use Pretty Links or your affiliate dashboard to track which content gets clicks.

- Which style got the most engagement?

- What platform worked best?

- Did people ask questions or DM you?

This is your blueprint.
The goal isn't to go viral — it's to go consistent.

Personal Example: Built from the Mess

When I relaunched everything — the books, the apparel, the site — I had to build affiliate income *around real life.*

No big budget.
No marketing team.
Just stories, simple systems, and tools I actually used.

I picked tools that helped me rebuild.
Then I told the truth about how they helped me —
one post at a time.

That's how this chapter was born.
Not from theory. From practice.

Final Words: Make It Repeatable

Affiliate content doesn't have to be complicated.
You don't need a new idea every day.

You need a system:

1. Choose the product

2. Create 3 types of content

3. Post, track, repeat

Do that every week with one new product?
You've got a scalable side income.

Content Planning Worksheet

Here's a simple table to help you start planning
weekly affiliate content.

Pick one product or tool per week.
Then build three styles of content around it (story, value, direct).
Post it. Track it. Repeat.

Chapter 9 – Real Affiliate Wins Take Time

We live in a world obsessed with *quick wins*.
Fast money. Viral moments. Instant gratification.
But affiliate marketing doesn't work like that — not if you want it to last.

This isn't about chasing clicks.
It's about building consistency.
It's about planting seeds — and giving them time to grow.

The $0 Phase Is Normal

You might post for a few weeks — and hear crickets.

That doesn't mean you failed. That's the warm-up.

Affiliate income doesn't always show up in real time.
People might save your post. Come back to it later.
They might not click your link until they actually *need* what you shared.

You're planting familiarity before you ever plant urgency.

Most of my early links didn't convert until weeks later.

But when they did, they stacked.

Consistency > Hype

You don't need to go viral. You need to stay visible.

One affiliate post per week — done consistently — beats a flood of hype posts that burn out your audience.

If someone sees you mention a product once? That's just a mention.

But if they see it 3–4 different ways over time —

in a story, a caption, a tools list, a real-life example —

that's when it becomes real.

> Repetition builds trust.
> Trust leads to clicks.
> And clicks lead to commissions.

Personal Story: Don't Be Me

I haven't always been the best at checking my affiliate dashboards.
Some programs offer bonuses. Some have tiered

payouts.
And if you're not paying attention, you might miss it all.

I've been surprised on more than one occasion — thinking I was getting a small payout, only to see something *way* bigger hit my account.

It was nice.
But it also reminded me: don't leave free money sitting on the table.

My Advice? Play the Long Game

The affiliate programs that change your income are the ones you *stick with*.

I've had payouts that hit months after the post.
Others that hit steadily every week because I built them into my systems.

> One of my Expedia payouts hit six weeks
> after I posted the link —
> long after I forgot about it.

You won't know which links will perform until you test them over time.
Don't quit early.

You're not just chasing traffic —

you're building trust.

And if you do that right?

You'll wake up to payouts you didn't even know
were coming —
because your content continues to work while you
sleep.

Final Thought

The money's there —
not in the rush,
but in the rhythm.

Build slow.
Build solid.
Stay steady when it's quiet.
Stay consistent when it's not.

Because those little coins?
They add up —
if your plan is built with purpose.

Chapter 10 – Stack, Test, Repeat

Affiliate income isn't just about posting links.
It's about building *layers* that quietly work for you over time.

One post is nice.

One payout is cool.

But real results come when you build a system you can stack.

Stack

You don't need 10 programs to get started.
You need **1–3 solid offers** that align with your brand, audience, or story.

Once those are in place, layer in your content:

- A post with your story around the product

- A blog or tools page for long-term traffic

- A weekly reminder (newsletter, podcast, episode recap, etc.)

- A visual or video walkthrough showing how you use it

- A saved highlight or pinned comment so it's always findable

That's stacking, not spamming.

You're building a *mini ecosystem* around each link.

Test

Everything won't work the first time.
Some links won't convert. Some posts won't hit.

That's okay.

You're not just an affiliate — you're a builder.
So *test like one*.

Try different:

- Headlines and angles

- Days and times

- Platforms and formats

- Ways of saying the same thing

Track what performs.
Tweak what doesn't.
And trust what works — even if it's not flashy.

Repeat

This is where the wins really happen.
Not in the "new," but in the **refinement.**

The best affiliate earners are boring with their discipline.

- They revisit old posts to update links

- They re-use what works in new formats

- They stay consistent, even when they're not inspired

Momentum compounds when you stop trying to outsmart it.

A Glimpse Ahead

I haven't hit it yet — but I know it's coming.

That week when three affiliate payouts hit —

not from luck, but from systems in sync.

That's not a dream.
That's discipline + time.

And that's the shift.
When it's no longer side income...
it's a second stream with structure behind it.

Final Thought

Don't overthink it.
Don't rush it.
Just stack.
Test.
Repeat.

You built this from scratch.
Now let it build for you.

From Me to You

I wrote this during a reset —

rebuilding my life, my business, and my belief in myself.

If you made it this far, you're not just reading — you're building too.

Keep going.
Keep testing.
I'll be right there with you.

BONUS TEMPLATES

For Builders Starting from Scratch

You don't need fancy software or a marketing degree to get started — just a few tools, clear goals, and a bit of consistency.

Use the resources below to organize your approach, plan your content, and treat your affiliate income like a business.

Content Planning Worksheet

Want the editable version?
Scan the QR code or visit:
heybbt.com/tools/affiliate-planner

Use it weekly.
If you stay consistent, the income will be too.

Caption Swipe File

Sometimes, the right line is all it takes to get someone to click.

I'm compiling my go-to captions, product callouts, and soft-sell hooks — so you can promote without sounding pushy.
→ Coming soon at Visit:
heybbt.com/tools/affiliate-planner

Builder's Tools Page / Linktree Strategy

Want to see how I organize and present affiliate links, tools, and offers in a clean, non-spammy way?

→ Visit: **heybbt.com/tools**

I'll keep that page updated with my latest layouts, software stack, and affiliate systems — so you can model what's working.

Acknowledgments

This book was written during a reset —
professionally, personally, and financially.

To those who checked in when I went quiet...
To the builders who kept showing up even when it
wasn't pretty...
To the creators who reminded me that value doesn't
need a spotlight...
Thank you.

You helped me remember what matters — and why
I keep building.

Always up.

— Brian